RAPS

drawings
by **LEN WESLEY**

Nelson-Hall Company
Chicago

RAPS

poems
by **ALFRED DUCKETT**

ISBN 0–88229–112–2

Library of Congress Catalog Card No. 73–77120

Copyright © 1973 by Alfred Duckett

For information address
Nelson–Hall Company, Publishers, 325 W. Jackson Blvd.,
Chicago, Ill. 60606.

Manufactured in the United States of America

DEDICATION

To the three Black Poets who influence me the most:
Langston Hughes, Owen Dodson and my dear sister,
Ruth Duckett Gibbs.

CONTENTS

COMMENT ON COMPLEXION

Everything you see walkin around

that ain't a one hundred percent Black job

is—you dig—some percent

shack job!

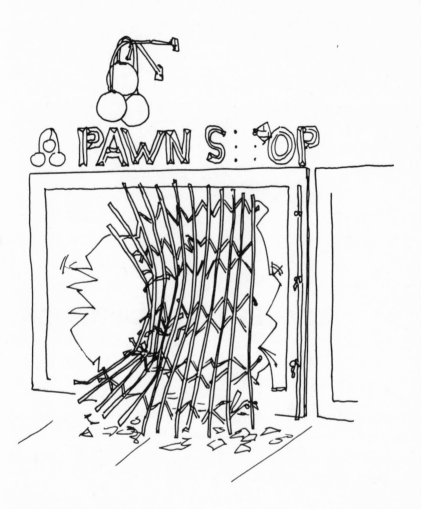

YOU CAN TELL ME

"Tell me, little brother!

"Tell me confidentially.

When you smashed that pawnshop window

and copped that color tv,

did you go to all that trouble

just so black folks could be free?

Tell me, little brother—

or you just like tv?"

3

I HEAR HARLEM

(A Dramatic Song Poem)

I hear Harlem
A wino's crazy jabber.
A greeting in the air
And slap of five to five.

"My main man! Where you been?"
And "How's the slave?"
And "How you and your woman making it?"
And "You still stay the same place?"

Because, in Harlem, there is shift
and change and breaking up and making up.
And it's a good trick to keep
the same job and the same old lady
and to live a lot of years under the same roof.

I hear Harlem
I hear the corner crowd
On liquid nights:
"Man, I'm tired of my gig."
Whitey get all the bread
And we the crumbs.
'Cause we ain't got the smarts
to stay in school.

5

And learn to play the game.
We filled with church talk
and woman talk and liquor talk.
We livin' in a marihuana mist.
We dying on our feet—but. . . . .

I hear Harlem too
of young and black and
self-reliant kids.
Of boys with Afro dos
and dashikas.

And girls who've learned
the elegance of black.
And kids who've learned
that slavery
is passe.
The slavery of now—yesterday.

A chorus over coffee:
"Remember when Malcolm said. . . . ."
Or "I didn't dig King
'til after he was dead."
We don't fare well
on welfare.
Farewell to welfare!
Dig it?"

"How much deeper can you bury soul
than on the dole?"

6

"How much cheaper can you buy a nigger—
and keep him sleep
than with welfare casework
and room and board and keep?"

And poverty programs!
They keep the middle class,
black bourgeoise
which does not care or dare or even
despair
about the black and poor and seething millions
of us in Harlem
and other Harlems
Like Beale Street
and Sunset and Vine
and Lee Street
and every cross the tracks
jukebox swinging
barbecue turning
likker-stinking
dope-dead
and dying
compound
acram
with millions of us black and poor and seething

Do you know what poor is
Poor is not paid on Friday
and broke Monday
And late with payment of living room set and

color tv
lighting up the slums
Poor is stomach ache
and mis-meal pains
and hearing babies cry
for not enough
of the stuff
that helps a baby not to die.

Poor is hand-me downs
brought home
And don't raise your voice to Mr. Charlie
Or he will cut off
the little bit of stuff
not quite enough
to feed all the mouths
in the sorry house.

Poor is war
to keep alive
to survive
Every and every and every day.

That's what I hear Harlem say

I hear Harlem
sneering at the dream
of integration
And a milk and honey world.
I hear Harlem demanding

No longer begging
Or marching or picketing
Or cooling it.
I hear Harlem say
"I'd rather be dead
than not have bread.
I'd rather burn
than yearn."

I hear black kids,
Vietnam-age,
consumed with rage
"I'd rather die."
And they don't lie.

I hear them say
Flying to the moon's
too soon
while earth is a mess
and happiness
is a thing not colored black.

I hear Harlem
bold and brave and tough
and thundering forth
that it is not enough
to measure freedom
by inches we have inched
to talk about the pinches
we have pinched
of freedom.

Freedom never can
be half-safe
Freedom is a man
who has the chance
to do the best he can

Freedom is no lift
Or gift

Freedom is either freedom
Or its not
And freedom is
What Harlem hasn't got

I hear Harlem
clearer every day

White man
Are you listenin?

10

FACE IT

No matter how
diddy bop
you walk . . .

Or how hard
you
street corner talk . . .

Brown boy.
Black boy.
You know better
than any other
that jail
with no bail
is a very
tough
mother!

HUH?

Hey,

Black parrott!

Black

pollyanna parrott

Black polly

want a

cracker?

want a graham

cracker?

Want a Billy

Graham

cracker?

ECONOMICS ONE

Some folks

Don't know you.

When

They owe you!

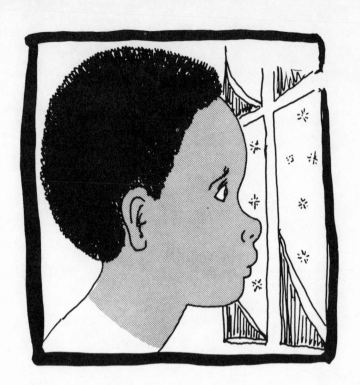

BLACK XMAS

Nobody had to tell

black kids

they ain't no sich as Santa.

They knew damn well

wasn't no white man

comin' to they neighborhood

late at night.

STEP ASIDE

Will you kindly step aside?
Pride
and making a living
and constantly giving.
Move out of the way.
What people say
and obligation
and reputation
and giving a damn
what people think I am.

I am—I know it.
A poet.

And I can sing
with a word.
Like a bird.
And I can laugh
and cry.
And I can put
my arms
around people
and make them know it.
I am a poet.
And a poet dares
because he cares
about people

with alarms,
who need arms
around them.

I need my own arms
around me.
I—who need
to be
a poet
and show it.

I cannot afford to die.
lips formed in the lie
of performing, conforming,
informing.

I want to stop here
beneath this tree
and see
this sun born.
And this sun be relieved
of duty
by that moon.
And this flower grow
And this rain tear glow.

I am a poet.
But you have to have
guts to be
a poet.

I want back my guts.

20

WHO? ME?

Me?

O. D?

Sheeee-ee, , , , ,

I'll tell you flat.

I'm much too cool for that.

I

don't intend to die.

See

I

dig me.

Do I mess with it?

A little bit.

But anytime I want to

I can quit.

No! I'm no saint.

But hooked I ain't.

Look here! I don't want to be a drag.

But could you lay a deuce on me for a bag?

Don't worry about a thing, my man.

I can quit. I really can.

22

WHAT SILENT MAJORITY?

They claim they polled the silent majority

and found a lot of folks that agree

with goddamn Vietnam.

Well, Charlie, they never polled me!

Anyhow

what make some fool think

no matter how foolish he be

that a pollstering man

can actually find

what's going through

some silent cat's mind?

They ain't got that thing together so good.

They ain't come into my neighborhood.

What old silent majority?

They ain't consulted Big Mouth. Me!

23

I'M BAD

A long shadow has fallen
    across my way.
A cold, chill breeze
    is ablowing today.
Birth is pretty and classic
    and pink.
Death is a fink, is a
    fink with a stink.
Professional hypocrites
    project death's beauty.
I fight ugly death; its
    a selfish duty.

Long shadow; cold chill
    go away.
I can bust your behind
    Any day.

Harlem (Trojan) Horse

WHITE IS THE COLOR

What color is "H?"
Why, white, of course.
White is the color,
of course,
of horse.

Who brings white "H."
meaning white hell,
into black Harlem?
You know quite well.

White men, of course,
bring in white horse
to poison for profit
black men, of course.

Black men. Dig?
But you can get it even quicker
if you're too young
to purchase liquor.

White men!
White horse!
Business is good
in the "black and
beautiful"
neighborhood.

SET DOWN, GAL

Little black woman!
You my queen.
I'm gonna buy you
another scene.

Gonna set you down
from fighting for me.
Huh! You think Lincoln
set you free?

Gonna buy you everything
a man's wife should have
when he's a king.

Set down, gal!

I don't mean wigs
or Cadillacs.
I don't mean the Quality
of Saks.

I don't mean
What Mrs. Whitey has
or what she do.
I mean I'm gonna buy you
your own black you!!

Set down, gal!
Set down, sweet, black gal!
Set!

30

HAIR

My good friend, Omar Ahmed said:

"It's easy enough to find

lots of soul folks with a natural head

and a very processed mind."

GOD BLESS JOHN WAYNE

I told my small
black friend
that he must not hold it
against
John Wayne
because
he is a cowman!
Man cow
who gives sour milk
from his udder brain.
Milk curdled with prejudice
and rancid with racism.

I told my small
and black and angry friend
that it is not totally
the fault
of John Wayne
that he has more muscle
than brain;
that he is a cowpuncher.
Cowpunchy
with oversize boyscoutism
and allegiance raving
and flag waving;
and that he is strange!

Mooing low discontent
with change.

That he is for mothers (white).
That he is a mother! Right?
A mother, beloved in mid-America region
and universally by the Legion.

I told my small
and hip and black
and angry friend
that John Wayne
will no longer reign
when America learns
it has become
much, much, much
too late
for the late, late
show.

34

BEWARE OF THE CAT

Don't think every black cat you see
is a Panther.

And don't make the mistake of believing
every non-Panther is a pussy cat.

35

WISH

Wish I had me a
woman
Like the woman I had
Swear to the Lord
I wouldn't treat her
     so bad
Wish I had a
     woman
To fuss with and
     fight
And cuddle up
     close to
Every night.

A woman could
     bake
     potato pie
And dance and sing
     with me
And get high
And be a angel
And be a slut
And sometimes—just
     sometimes
Keep her mouth shut.

Want me one, pretty

and neat
Cats go to whistling
When she come
     down the street.

They eyes can shine
They teeth will
     grit
But none of my
     woman
Can they git.

Wish I had a woman
Like the woman I
     had
Swear to Jehovah
I wouldn't treat
     her bad.

I sure wish.

38

FAMILY ADVICE

Brothers!

More think

Less Drink

More Hope

Less Dope

Brothers!

Less rap

Less nap

More cool

And school

That equals

Making it

Taking it.

Dig?

LA VIE

A little wave came and kissed my legs
and rippled on away.
A middle-sized wave washed in on me
and seemed inclined to stay.
Another wave, puppy-playful, came
and slapped me in the chest
and knocked me down—and silly me,
I liked that one the best.

LET'S BE *YOUNG LOVERS*
(For the late Whitney Young, Jr.)

Before the eye is dry;
the shock old;
the gratitude cold—
Let us say
"Thank you" today
To a man who was bold

To a man
Who made a choice
Between an angry voice
And a workable plan.

To a man who walked with kings
Bearing a torch for the lowly
To a man whose dedication
Was a bright flame
Almost holy.

Let's not shed tears
That will dry all too fast.
Let's work through the years
For his work to last.

Let's be Young lovers.
Not fickle or afraid
to widen the path
of the trail he made.

SONNET

Where are we to go when this is done?
will we slip into old, accustomed ways,
finding remembered notches, one by one?
Thrashing a hapless way through quickening haze
Who is to know us when the end has come?
Old friends and families perhaps, but could we be
strange to the sight and stricken dumb
at visions of some pulsing memory?
Who will love us for what we used to be
who now are what we are, bitter or cold?
Who is to nurse us with swift subtlety,
back to the warm and feeling human fold?

Where are we to go when this is through?
We are the war-born. What are we to do?

A BLACK MAN'S PRAYER

God, teach me to be a Black man . . . to know what a Black man is supposed to be. You've got a reason for everything. You had one for making me.

God, teach me to ask what a Black man is. I can only ask it of me. I can only ask it when I realize You have a reason for me.

A Black man is simply another man . . . like another man who is white. That's what I say . . . but often, I don't act like I believe I am right.

Sometimes, I act like I'm different. Like I'm special and think I should get some special sort of treatment . . . like a freak or a cherished pet. Sometimes, I act like I'm trying to PROVE . . . the evil some men say of me . . . and expect to be forgiven and treated with sympathy.

God, teach me to learn that I must live . . . as other folks are living. Teach me that I have to give . . . as other folks are giving.

The good they are and the good they do. Is what I must do and be. The bad in them I must learn to shun . . . and the good I must use for me.

I must be proud to be a Black man. And, if others hate my hue . . . I must not be angry . . . but pity them because they do not know You.

And I must not ONLY pity them. I must win them to me with love. And, holding their hands in mine, I must point to your rainbow up there above.

I must make them see Your rainbow glow . . . all its colors in harmony. By word and deed, I must let them know the thing You have told to me.

That the loveliest sight in the Heavens is a blend of colors diverse and the rainbow itself is a promise that things will be better . . . not worse.

God, teach me to be proud as a Black man. Proud . . . that Creation Day . . . You hollowed your hand to make me of the RICHEST dark of clay. You fashioned me for sorrow and you fashioned me for joy. You gave me a dream for tomorrow and taught me that pain can't destroy.

I know, God, You're a just God. I suspect your purpose with me. Was to help You teach my brothers how men ought to worship Thee. But, before I can teach, I must learn, God. And all I can learn here below . . . is that You are the only lasting Truth and that there is nothing else I know.

"Those He loves, He chastiseth." The Bible puts it that way. God teach me to learn this lesson and to repeat it from day to day.

God, teach me to be understanding . . . after your own design. Teach me to see another's point of view although it conflicts with mine.

God, teach me to be courageous . . . and when I stand firm for a right. Let me be defending not only myself, but championing with all my might . . . the rights You've decreed for all mankind. Yes, even my enemy. Let my enemy be my foe, if he must, but keep alive in me . . . the greatest force on all the earth and even beyond Your sky . . . the force of love for my fellow-man . . . a force that can never die.

God teach me to be humble; that to be humble is not to be weak. To be humble is to be strong that when others threateningly speak . . . so great is my faith in your promise, so rich my security . . . that I do not have to say what I am. All I have to do is be.

God, teach me to be generous. Teach me that there is no school which can give me the wisdom I can find in life's own golden rule.

God, teach me to have faith as a Black man . . .
to know when people say . . . I am less than what I
should be . . . I am just as much . . . no more . . . than
they. I must never give back scorn for scorn or hate for
hatred's curse. I must learn to know how to take a blow
without having a wound to nurse.

I must know You are the Healer. I must know that
I know not all. I must know that each God-man is
important . . . each God-man, big or small. I must
know that You with a purpose .·. . with a well-con-
sidered plan; for everyone . . . black, white, rich or
poor . . . in all the world of Man.

God, teach me to be a Black man . . . with PRIDE
and DIGNITY. With love for my brother and faith in You
and with deep humility.

God, teach me to be a Black man.

OUT OF THE MOUTHS

My godson, seventeen,
normally nonchalant
regarding political follies,
refers to Mr. Nixon as
"the cat who has no jellies."

WHAT'S YOUR EXCUSE?

White cop in the Harlem riot.

Told me "Go home," tossing his head

I looked him deep in his cold, blue eyes.

"I'm home, baby," I said.

THE DUKE

Duke Ellington's music

almost came too soon.

A gaunt coyote

Keening at the moon.

Mighty organ waters

rushing to the sky

and a great broad,

passing by.

Duke Ellington's music.

A noonday dream.

A secret joke.

Pure cream.

A train gone crazy

on a wide open track.

Bitter-strong

like coffee,

hot and black.

56

SATURDAY NIGHT UPTOWN

On Saturday night
life is cheap
in the ghetto.

Cousin from Jackson, Miss.
who scraped his feet
and bowed his head
for Mr. Charlie,
He bad in the ghetto
on Saturday night.

Back home, he was heartless afraid
of Mr. Charlie.
But he kill his black brother.
Instant death.
Over a pint of third class wine.

At Harlem Hospital,
on Saturday night,
a cut-up cat
or a shot up woman,
just another incident.

Life real cheap in the ghetto
on Saturday night.

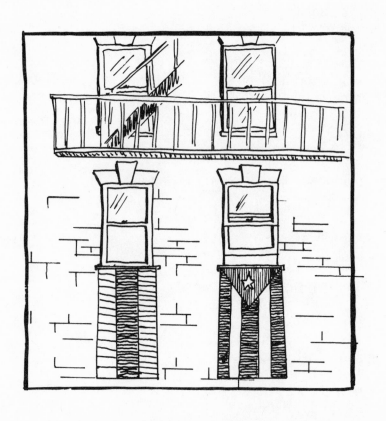

CONSPIRACY

Used to be a time
white man could say
to an innocent black man:
"You okay.

"But nix on them spicks
They not good as you.
They work cheaper.
Then you'll be through."

Used to be a time
white man could say
to innocent Porto Rican:
"You okay.

"But niggers ain't no good
They don't want you in they neighborhood."

That was usta time.
But its different today.
Black and brown power
going the same way.

Division ain't cool
you will sure enough find
when it means dividing up
mankind.

WHAT HARLEM IS TO ME

Here's what Harlem is to me.
Brittle branch on a spreading tree.
Isle of exile.
Isle of joy.
A place of agony and joy.

Here's what Harlem is to me.
Juke mills, live with sounds and gin.
Savoy—where lithe, young bodies spin.

Here's my Harlem—a cathedral tall.
A storefront, smaller than a stall.
A wise, old church with dignity.
The sob of preaching ecstasy.

Here's what Harlem is to me.
Tired maid mother, coming home.
A teen aged jean-teen, little gnome-
seeking chills and thrills and love.
This, my Harlem is made of.
Weary.
Old, young father.
Postal clerk, Superintendent, Soda jerk.
Doctor, lawyer, hustler too.
West Indian, Moslem and Black Jew.

Garbage, stinking up the hall.

Kids whose bodies are too small.
A debutante ball.
A fraternity.
That's what Harlem is to me.

Long lines of kids and grown-ups too.
Outside the theatre.
Long, long queue waiting to delight the soul
with the greatest rock and roll.

Chamber music at the Y.
Student enraptured with Hi-Fi.

Red, racy cars.
Snoot limousines.
Barbecue.
Hog fat and beans.
Pigs feet, bubbling in the pot.
Jackie Robinson coffee, piping hot.
Caviar.
Chop suey.
Cod.
Chicken fried—so good, my God!
Hot dogs, bursting from the roll.
Home-made pies and casserole.

Tenements—where rats live free.

That's what Harlem is to me.

Gracious homes with gracious lights.
Tight, little apartments.
Walk five flights.
Knock on any door and find—different people
different mind.
Different ambitions.
Different desires.
Different vices.
Different fires.
Progressive trio.
A symphony.
That's what Harlem is to me.

Walled-in Harlem—on its own.
Left to find its way alone.
But, come to Harlem—Oriental or white.
Harlem never gives you spite.
Harlem gives you outstretched hand.
Same hand you bruised.
Gee, Harlem's grand.
Harlem believes enslavers should be free.
And that's why Harlem's great for me.

Here's what Harlem means, you see.
Mirror of society.
Mocking mirror—giving back—laughter—
high yellow, brown and black.
Yes, laughter and tap steps and cries of joy.
But Harlem's no longer a shuffling boy.
No hat in hand.

No shoulders hunched.
Harlem's the reason Joe Louis punched.
And Ray Robinson danced in a squared-off ring—
and looked like a glorious, panther thing.
And Harlem's why black boys and brown boys too.
Went off to fight for red, white and blue.

And some came back.
And some would have been better—if the War
Department had sent a letter.

No, Harlem's no longer a shuffling boy.
The city's back yard where businessmen find joy—
by bribing a native to produce his sister.

Harlem's grown up—a man now, mister.

Harlem is good and Harlem is bad.
And Harlem has everything any place ever had.
Crap shooters, cab drivers, preachers and pimps.
Men who are giants and men who are shrimps.
Men who are bitter and men who are cruel.
Women who are learned or who play the fool.
Whores and hussies and women like flame.
Sunday School teachers and social workers and
none the same.

Harlem has muscles, flexing to be free.
Harlem has bright eyes, glued on democracy.
Harlem is royal and loyal and foul.
And bright as a sparrow—and drab as an owl.

But an owl is wise—up there in his tree.

And Harlem is wise, mister—take it from me.

FOR HER PEOPLE

(To Gwen Brooks)

Never met the lady.
But she's a lady, I know.
And I can tell
she's a woman also.
Black man's woman.
Not only fine.
But she also been putting
those dues on the line.

Mischief in her poetry.
Brown sugar laughs.
And absolute soul
in them photographs.
For her people
She wrote beautiful things.
For her people
her heart sings.

Never met the lady.
Heard my friend Era Bell say
She's shy, down and cool
and A-OK.
Never really had the pleasure.
'Cept in books.
And I came to testify
that Gwendolyn Brooks

COOKS!

Alfred Duckett

Poet, author, editor, and lecturer, Alfred Duckett has been a writer for over 35 years.

At present he is editorial director of **Equal Opportunity Magazine,** which he co-founded in 1969, and a director of Associated Negro Press International.

Previously he was associate editor of **Ebony** and **Negro Digest** (now **Black World**), and was a reporter and columnist on **Afro-American, Pittsburgh Courier, Chicago Defender, New York Age,** and **Amsterdam News.** For five years he was ghostwriter for the late Jackie Robinson's syndicated column.

He wrote two books with Jackie Robinson, **Breakthrough to the Big Leagues** and **I Never Had It Made.** He also is author of **The Changing Guard—The New Black Political Breed.** His poetry has been published in **Poetry of the Negro,** edited by Langston Hughes and Arna Bontemps; **American Negro Poetry,** edited by Arna Bontemps; **Afro-American Poetry,** edited by June Jordan; and **Twice-A-Year Anthology,** edited by Dorothy Norman.